LISTENING TO LEADING

Ramesh Sood

My Prayer!

Thank you, God
for giving me wings to fly.
Give me courage, and
Humility to let me
keep my feet on the earth.

Dear Reader,

Nothing in life is complicated which cannot be explained in simple day to day words. This is an experiment done by me.

I wonder if I have been successful in saying it all in minimum words.

A senior professional read it and said, "I am feeling strange. Magical this! None can say it in a simpler way. Publish it." And I did. It took me 20 years.

I dedicate this book to my parents who watch me from above and keep sending their blessings. I shall always remain thankful to my family who continue to practice a lot of patience as within moments, I would be there but not there often getting lost in my thoughts...

It is my hope that you will appreciate the simplicity with which this book is written, created and presented to you.

Ramesh Sood

Pune.

Welcome!

Here we go! I have one request. Do take a pause after reading the verse. Think and contemplate. You will enjoy and like it better. I am hopeful. Happy Reading!

CONTENTS

LISTENING

I can keep on talking and talking
for endless hours without a blink;
but listening is so hard & tiring
I'm almost always on the brink.

Because I evaluate, I judge,
I perceive differently.
I want to show my superiority.
I want to have an edge over you.

TRUST

When I trust you and share all my thoughts,
I don't expect a betrayal even in my dream,
And if you do, nothing much would happen, you
would mean less than a human being.

That's about it.
I can't shift my value.
I will continue to trust.
You won't be there with me.
I will become stronger.

PERCEPTION

For me, a bird may mean just a flight
and you may perceive it as joy and freedom;
if we accept just this difference
what a lovely relationship it would become!

Yes, we give meaning to things based on our Maps of Reality. Like I can't find paths of your mind by looking at my map. I will have to understand your map. For that, I must give you time. And know that both the maps are different.

PREDICTABILITY

If I find you pretty consistent
in your behavior and all the actions
and if you aren't strong deep inside then I may
play with your reactions.

If I know what makes you angry, what irritates you,
what pleases you, what upsets you and what truly
makes you angry or happy or joyous then I can
choose your behavior along with mine.
So take care friend!

DECEPTION

To win him over for a while
I gave him a big false smile;
my smile faded as I realized, alas!
My whole being had become false.

Sometimes we don't say what exactly we feel.
We exchange false smiles which do not have their
roots in our heart or soul but stem from the mind.
And it becomes a habit as the years pass by.
Trouble is that the gesture remains the same even
when one stands in front of the mirror.

INSPIRATION

Obstacles are plenty, yet I'll move
One step at a time, soft and slow
None may notice and hold me back
I know as a tree, slowly I'll grow.

Growing slowly is always helpful.
Trees do not grow in one day.
They take years to grow.
And then they grow with strong roots, a very strong
stem and fruits and shade for all.
Yes, I won't mind growing like a tree.

GOAL

To reach my goal, if I go on changing path
How would I ever know how did I reach?
I am on my path and shall stay on it
And let my goal be wherever I may reach.

When one gets hooked with or obsessed with some material goal, then one wants to achieve it at any cost. One keeps on changing one's path. Then reaches and wonders about one's footprints. Can we stay on our path to reach wherever we do – leaving behind clear marks and footprints if anyone chooses to follow.

POWER

The powerful commands
As the lesser ones bow,
With the passage of time
.... All of them go.

Oh, the moment you are bestowed with power,
you want to use it! You want to use it unabashedly
and sometimes mercilessly. You want to command
the lesser-ones. Yes, because they are there to serve
you. Nothing much changes as the world keeps on
moving and the lesser ones continue to curse.

SUCCESS

Reaching the top of the ladder
If that's the success,
Then those holding the ladder?
Poor souls; God bless!

You say that you are successful because it's
you who reached the top of the ladder.
But then you have reached the top supported by
some people who chose to hold the ladder for you;
And in a way, they too succeeded. But why then only
you alone are termed as 'successful'?

PROCRASTINATION

I knew I could,
I thought I would,
Then should I or shouldn't,
Time flew and I couldn't.

And I said with real passion in my voice, "I will
pursue this and show to the world that I can do it."
My friend who perhaps knew me better than I could
ever know myself made his usual comment,
"You can do it, but you will not." Prophetic words
those! I proved him right. I just didn't start.

RAPPORT

Cactus and Rose lived happily together
With the blessings of soil, wind and Sun
No fights, no jealousies, simple love,
None tried to make others like the one.

A gift of acceptance. They have accepted each other the way they are. Rose doesn't want the cactus to become a rose and the cactus doesn't want the rose to be like it. That's it! Simple. But is it that simple? Will we the human ever learn from nature?

PERSISTENCE

On every failure, I would lose my heart,
I would curse, crib and keep on crying,
Then a wise guy told me to always persist
I learnt to succeed by relentlessly trying.

We always start things with a bang. Making a lot of
noise and claiming a hundred percent success in a
very short period of time. With time we lose steam.
Something happens. We just have to be relentless.
The torch of hope will have to be kept ablaze.
We must persist.

TEAM WORK

Relentlessly pursuing a common goal
When everyone does his own bit
Giving hundred per cent, extending help
If that's not Team Work then what's it?

Each one plays their role to perfection. And helping others in the team. What fantastic team-work, that! In the word TEAM hide two more words: Tame & Mate

DEPENDABILITY

Sun rates Moon high on 'Dependability',
For he always comes in time for the Night,
And never tries to shine when it's Sun's turn,
Happily, the sun too gives him all his light.

My goodness! So true it is. Just put "Boss' in place
of Sun and you become ' Moon' for a minute. And
try to do with your Boss what Moon does with Sun.
Lo, behold! You are able to solve all your problems
with your boss. That's what perhaps every Boss asks
himself - Can I depend on this person?

ATTITUDE

So what if I couldn't reach ashore,
No, my dream hasn't turned sour,
Well, I can start absolutely afresh,
Burying the past & moving ahead.

It happens all the time. Some succeed and find their dreams getting fulfilled. Some don't and feel shattered. I will like to remember one quote from "Illusions" by Richard Bach in which he says – "If you wish to know whether your mission on earth is over, then if you are alive, it is not."

HARD WORK

Hard work pays,
As the hard-working grows,
When others crib,
One smiles, for, one knows.

Hard work pays. Smart work pays as well but in the short run. Nothing can replace Hard Work for success in the long run. And those who have been successful in their lives, their biographies would tell whether they worked hard or not. You, the illumined soul, keep on working hard.

FOUNDATION

Devotion, Dedication and Desire,
Picking up these traits became my goal,
When I sought advice, the wise-one said,
"Just go and get in touch with your soul."

Wisdom of elders revealed that if I wanted to be focused, dedicated and devoted to fulfill my own desire to succeed in life, I would have to look deep within to cleanse my inner-space. I realized over the years of unsuccessful attempts the value of self-discipline, self-control and focus.

DELEGATION

He was ignored for a push upward,
For none below could be elevated,
And that's when he realized the truth,
If only he could have 'delegated'.

If I want to climb higher then I will have to move from the place where I stand today. Which means what I do at my present place, someone else will have to do it i.e I will have to delegate. If I do it myself then I am not delivering my value. This is what happens. People continue to grow without making organizations grow.

SELF-REALISATION

Whenever I tried to show
How big I was,
In those moments, perhaps
I was acting very small.

Big people are of two kinds: Those who are made and those who become big. Those who are made are not of much concern to our sensibilities but those who become big with their efforts can manifest their success in their behaviour either by becoming humble or by showing off. Choose.

RECOGNITION

He patted my back when we were alone
And I knew that it was just his appreciation,
When with courage he did it in front of all,
How I loved it for I knew it was recognition!

How difficult and extra ordinary, this! Recognising something good by openly praising to make one not only feel enhanced but also leave one happier and deeply satisfied indeed works wonders. Such recognition gives birth to passion and loyalty among people–two most essential professional traits.

BOSS

Boss is a reality,
You can't do away;
Accept and adjust
or just go away.

"Fine, I have heard you. Your thoughts are very good. Keep For now do what I want you to do. I expect you to finish the task by tomorrow." A boss is a boss is a boss. Whichever way the coin may fall, heads or tail, it's always the boss who will win the toss. It's for the real. Accept it.

SELF-AWARENESS

To go to the darkest corners
Of my inner space, I dare,
It's this fearlessness, perhaps,
That makes me "Self Aware".

Most of us always like to know ourselves only through our brighter side. We need to look at our darker corners too for we deserve our own forgiveness. Let us then be courageous to take that inward journey sooner than later. That's when darkness withers away to give way to light.

BEING ALIVE

If I haven't learnt today
Then I haven't grown
Then I haven't lived
Then am I or am I not?

They say that at some stage body stops growing. It starts getting disintegrated as we move through life. We still keep living. But then for any living thing growth has to necessarily happen. So we must grow in mind. Not learning then will mean – A lifeless living.

TRAINER/COACH

He holds my finger and takes me along,
After a few steps asks me to walk alone,
Shows me the path; cheering me up,
Also gifting me with a desire to move on.

Christa McAuliffe once said, "I touch future. I teach." Same is with a Trainer or a Coach who gives whole-heartedly. It's up to us to receive. For none can give you if you don't want to receive. That's where the trick lies. An effective trainer/ coach also lights that spark in you that creates a hunger to receive.

VICTORY?

Winning many a battle I reached the top
Like stepping stones many heads I used
When in vacant moments I met with my soul,
Oh! She was badly battered and bruised.

Mind loves to use people for its own benefit and keeps on hurting the Soul which remains a mute spectator. And man losing touch with his soul, continues with his own manipulative behaviour. Then one day when he comes face to face with the soul, well, he would be lucky to recognize it.

HAPPINESS

So happy I was in my joyful present
When from my unpleasant part of past
Don't know why I invited a thought,
And alas! My happiness couldn't last.

Ah! To receive all the accolades from every one! Then
to wait for acknowledgment from that one person
who had always ignored. Receiving his attention
had become an obsession. Mind would pick up a
bad mood out of habit. I learned and pushed the
unwanted out. You can too.

FRIENDSHIP

It's not that I don't want a friend
It's only that I can't pretend
If you are real without a mask
Just say it you don't have to ask.

While growing up we all get in to the habit of giving
lot of importance to labels. We refuse to look at
that thin line between flattery and sincerity. False
friendships based on the needs grow. Let us be real.
Two mask-less people! How beautiful it can be? Let's
try. What do you think?

ACCEPTANCE

I fell in love with a flower
But then what about root and stem
and branches, soil and the leaves
how can I ignore all of them?

People fall in love. Get together. And then slowly
the realisation that there are others attached to each
other. Conflicts. Breakups. Why? Love the plant.
Flower exists because of the roots, stem, soil and
surrounding. Because of them, it is what it is - worthy
of your love. Think!

MIND

Just focuses on the external noise,
and politely shuns the inner voice.
No confusion and no turmoil,
mind often makes an easier choice

Mind loves playing, making mess of things and calculating. It's so easy. Doesn't like to get in touch with the heart lest it starts getting influenced. Making heart suffer is also a game of the mind. Don't let your heart fall a prey to the games of the mind. Beware of that stress!

ADAPTABILITY

New soil would always resist
Seed must adapt & go through the pain;
when roots develop and stems grow
then God too showers all the rain.

I remember having left the place of my birth and made another one my new home. Took me time to get that I had joined the people there. They hadn't joined me. So onus of developing rapport was on me and not on them. From that point onwards a new journey began that is still continuing.

DIRECTION

One may feel one's moving ahead
Yet may not enjoy fruits of action
For one may be totally ignorant that one's yet to
find the right direction.

It happens. With our own limited understanding
of the things we keep on making efforts thinking of
delicious fruits which elude us. Not that something
is lacking in our efforts. It's only that we are not yet
tuned up with our passion. You will get there. Stay
focused and alert.

PERSEVERANCE

So what if I couldn't reach ashore,
No, my dream hasn't turned sour.
Well, I can start absolutely afresh,
Burying the past & moving ahead.

It happens all the time. Some succeed. Some don't. I remember one quote from "Illusions" by Richard Bach in which he says – "If you wish to know whether your mission on earth is over, then if you are alive, it is not." This one lesson has made me persevere and persist. Hopefully!

MANAGING HUMAN RESOURCE

Everyone works to fulfill their dreams,
Doesn't matter the caste, creed or religion
Whenever you need to reprimand or reward
Oh, please know this: HR = Heart + Reason

He was sitting in front of his manager. Teary eyed.
Emotional. A fresh Graduate Engineering Trainee.
Had to leave home to work. Only son of his father.
In spite of lack of resources, father had ensured to
get him to college. Boy was missing him. Wanted
to be with him. Everyday phone was not possible.
There were no mobiles. Wanted to leave. Was firm.
His manager picked up the phone without warning,
dialed his father's number, told his father about the
reality. Father pleaded to make him stay. Manager
gave the phone to boy. And voila! A couple of
moments. The boy started smiling. Reason wanted
him to stay. Heart pushed him to go. He balanced
them. Manager helped him balance them by keeping
the right balance himself. Yes, Heart +Reason win the
day any day.

LEADERSHIP

He guided me, showed me the path,
For some distance he walked along
Then one day just pushed me from behind
"It's your journey now, it's your song."

When I was little, I would follow my father holding his finger. When I grew up, he asked me to walk besides him. After some more years, he would make me walk ahead of him. I learned to keep an eye behind. Then one day I was walking alone.

Leadership is about being in the front when the leaders under you are still developing, beside them when they are grown up and willing to pave their own path, and behind when you know they are moving firmly on their own, and invisible to let them start developing new set of leaders.

Hello Friend,

Greetings!

Thanks for giving me the greatest honour by reading this experimental book.

Trust you found it useful. Has this book helped you?

In that case do pass a word to your friends.

I wish you all the best.

Ramesh Sood,

Ramesh Sood is a Pune based Experienced Life Coach, Trainer and a Richard Bandler Certified Master Practitioner of NLP. He has trained over 3000 people from various segments. Has been a panellist and a guest speaker in many a forum. Before this he has written Five Books which came from deep contemplation of his life's experience. Ramesh has also written about 380 articles and 2000 plus daily posts on LinkedIn, He has more than 34000 discerning minds as committed readers.

Wrote a Saturday Feature which was being published in Popular Marathi Daily Sakal from Jan. 2019 till Dec. 2020.

Received Highest Recognition in College & Corporate. Played TT at National Level.

A poet who also received an award as Haiku King in 2012 after winning a month-long Haiku Challenge. His poetry blog has about 1100 posts.

Ramesh Says: Whenever I want to think aloud, I write!

His hashtag defines his work, simple yet effective.

#simplySOOD

www.simplysood.com